POETRY MANIA

By Nickle Smith

YOU ARE

He walked right in like he owned the place,
A broad shouldered Joe with a hero's face

He knew what he was after from the moment he sauntered by.
Antiques were looming everywhere,
but he knew he had to try.

He grabbed the gals attention and looked her in the eye,
Then pointed to a dusty item they'd hidden way up high.

His voice was gruff with confidence as he poised himself to say,
"That's the one for me lady love-I'll take her home today".

Her lip curled up as she responded with
complete and utter disgust
"Sir I'm sure you've chosen wrong
that one is cracked and gathering dust".

"In all the years I've had it-it never got used once
I can't believe I've left it out-I'm really such a dunce.
The quality of our items is much too high to sell a piece like that.

Now that I'm aware of it, its going to the back".

The man dismissed her ramblings and
retrieved the piece on his own.

Once the dirt was wiped away he knew what he'd been shown

Tears streamed down his weathered face as he
read the two words that remain,

And for a simple moment this nothing eased his pain.

The woman interrupted-"There used to
be a set of them which read:

You are what you eat

I don't see why you'd want it now-

it's not even complete".

He knew there was no way to explain that after
years of searching near and far

The closest thing he'd found of truth is this
damaged plate exclaiming,

YOU ARE.

HEAVY NOTES

Lyrics keep me company while I'm traipsing through my memory. My thoughts entangle and hum with the beat as the notes cleanse the chaos in them. If these lines are all I have to disappear into then I will memorize every last one as if they were the constellations in heaven.

Fixed yet free.

PEEK A BOO

Crawl inside this darkness with me, round and round the clock
with vacancy in our eyes we'll ride the ride until it's time to fly.

I've lost my mind and closed my heart. The blood
flows warm but it's black as black and the void
grows bigger in the absence of your light.

COTTON BALL

My heart is ruptured, and I've plugged it with could-be's and weren'ts and now it's sprung a leak which can't be held back. I haven't shed a tear in so long that they burn my cheeks as they slide down my face now. I want to go back to the way it was when the hole was plugged tight, when I couldn't remember what it felt like to be clogged with all this thickening sickening emotion.

I just want to go back.

DEMONS THAT DANCE

I"ve pondered on it for long enough, it's painfully obvious I yearn for the torture. That ache which comes from nowhere else, a prisoner to a thing that's never been mine. Cursing the euphoria and its mere discovery. What a devastating thing to let slip through weak hands...

I'd rather scald the skin than numb the sensations. Wouldn't I?

MUSTARD SEED

It's irrevocable to reveal that which remains hidden in
the depths of a universe I've locked down so tightly.

To catch even a glimpse of the weight of souls buried there
have crushed the mountain like pinecones under boot.

The mountain is glorious, discerning and full
of dark jagged caves; I found myself lost in it
when I dared not elevate on my own.

So, which is the kindness of now? Is it to honor the mountain
and infinitely tend to these promises for the gift of love,
protection and stability it alone has provided; Or shall
I simply glide solitary through the sea discovering all
which is wavering or unknown without hesitation?

As if once more a mere pebble, just the me that I used to be...

SPRAY PAINT

I couldn't be anyone else even if I expertly clawed
and fought my way out of this brain, and believe
me, I have tackled the task before.

Building houses over tombstones in graveyards of my
head is simply a reaction. The flowers planted there won't
wither and can't die. Often it baffles me, all the awful racket
up there gave life to the spunky gardens down here.

I think I'll lie there for awhile and pretend the petals are
clouds, cuddled up in the cosmos; not rooted to ground...

WHAT BOX?

A well-balanced soul mustn't be restrained or possessed. Rather shared and protected with the priceless rarities who possess the eye to appreciate it's wonder and enhance it with their own.

This is love.

Not to hurt or compete nor to gain steps ahead. To be there when the hurt ones need to be loved and the lonely one's cry for their pain. That is a selfless love.

An act most kind.

HOW ARE YOU, ARTIST?

Frankly I've become exhausted; I'm unable to conjure my creativity. But, if this day I choose not write, the thoughts will remain trapped in me all through the night.

LEISURE

I relish this time i find to myself; I can be only me and nobody else.

SPRINKLER SYSTEMS

I prefer to remain trapped in my backyard than buried in yours.
At least here, the grass keeps green year-round.

BINGE WATCHING

The thought police are on my case. Trudging through the muck of madness left in the wake of us all trying to "figure it out". What is there to figure when the problems are all beyond comprehension to me and were solved for eternities before you anyways? Now, that's a question, none of this who am I, what does it all mean babble. Out and out facts that's what I'll take if anyone's got them. But you know what they say, wish in one hand...we're all a pile of what-ifs and what is, and nobody knows how to be an EVERYTHING. Looking down upon the floundering masses, flabbergasted by our refusal to embrace the fact there is no measure of time. Once the secret's out, repetition revealed and the hope of "someday" taken away, would we all still play the game? I guess we'll "figure it out"...

SOMEDAY.

SHADOWISMS

Stressing obsessing over tasks unmet and toils not toiled. My mind a mess of unhappenings amidst the imminent reality of which if I'm honest, will pass with such a quickness that when these tasks have gone, I'll hardly think of them at all. I'll be trapped again in a cage of my making, insecurities abound here, and I've learned to befriend the shadows of myself, if only for now, to not feel so forgotten.

So far from who I was and what I wanted from myself. A gift only I can recover and yet I'm trying to hand it to you, whilst clawing at my chest for it to stay. Begging, yet again.

Stay tucked in the cage these ribs have built, safe and beating against walls that can only bring death if it finally breaks them down. So i sit in my mind, in the sky where I'll watch them. Observe the mistakes we'll be making for eternity, hiding myself and whispering sweet hopelessness to ever present shadows who do not appear without their light.

ADRIFT

I am an island, one if by sea, a simple creation in solitary.

Waves relentlessly attack, eroding white sands,
scrubbing away what's left of my hands.

Fruitless flares dissipate, unseen in the sky, a
deafening silence their only reply.

MOODY

SMILE the SMILE that lasts for awhile

Embracing the flow of my inner love's glow

SPIRALING quickly to a place down below

SOBBING the sobs that let everyone know

Swing-in 29 words

There are many ways to SWING-unfortunately, our MOODS arent exempt from this lovely action... at least mine aren't today.

AN EYE WITH WHICH WE SEE

I am the EYE that peeks for TRUTH, gazing at the WHY with
that analyzing EYE, hoping for depth and magic and MORE

YOU are the THEM who complicate and multiply, scattering
like insects in the presence of a larger SOMETHING

A WE that herds and marches blindly and endlessly
toward an omnipotent ONE to reward the tears and
toy soldiers falling and fighting in LINE

I am the EYE that burns for truth, welding my parts
into pieces and burning desperately to be WHOLE

I am MY thoughts MY fantasies MY wrinkles
of TIME and THOUGHT

Blending knowledge and EXPERIENCE and dreaming of ME

The ME I see when my eyes are squashed tight and
IMAGINE the most FANTASTICAL self

I am the EYE weeping for the WE that only the EYE can SEE

Gazing into an INFINITY of WE and YOU and THEM

I am the ME that I MADE ME to be-a THOUGHT that was a
seed and watered by my TEARS and YEARS and TRIALS

An ENTITY of molecules and genomes smashed
and crashed and BONDED to THEY

Millions of MINDS that seek what was
SOUGHT and wonder the WHY'S

MYSELF is the SELF I aimed to be before
there was YOU or HE or US

LIGHT the dark and dilate YOUR heart and soul in SEARCH of I

Creating the MOMENTS that make up my NOW and
yesterday; a perception perceived in DREAMS

I AM THE EYE

*Where would we be without thought and misery and fantasy-
it is me and it was THEM. The artists and thinkers who
THOUGHT and GRIEVED and aspire to more...*

ACID RAIN

Is this how it feels to be pushed from the nest? Shivering in the
chill of loneliness-heart shards stabbing through my chest?

Once I was warmed by the light of a loyal beam, maneuvering
with the grace of millions-part of a royal team.

Divinity has darkened me; dropped me from on high, and thus an

angel lost her wings, and plummeted from the sky.

Curse the Cosmos! Defile your sweet name! For now
I am filthy and splattered with shame.

GUARDIAN

She grew weary of people and their chaotic emotion,

So she wished for a swing in the midst of the ocean.

Each day she was greeted by the warmth of the sun;

Serenaded by sea gulls as the evening was done.

A patchwork of twinkling stars to keep her heart aglow;

Forever pumping higher to leave the pain below.

Still each day she watches all her loved ones from afar,

and if you're really lucky, you'll catch her swinging from a star.

THE RISE

Our souls mingle in silky seduction until
at last, achieving ERUPTION.

Contest prompt: one line on Euphoria

REPLACEABLE

I stood frozen in front of you;

Gazing at the jagged rocks below, waves assaulting Earth.

I stood silent in front of you;

Plucking my petals one by one
as they flutter toward the abyss.

I hovered peacefully above;

My body floating lifeless, a black rose swept away at sea.

SOUL SURRENDER

Salt sickens my saliva as I swallow my simple soul;
Slicing simplicity into spoiled spaces and secret speeches.

Surrendering my sorrows to surreptitious sellers of solace;
Selling sex, substance and security.

Shattering sweet slumbers of sincerity and serenity;
Sweeping me onto this
sinking ship, as I slowly submerge,
Suffering into the nothing.

SMOG

My heart is heavy, for the present is bleak;
Dealing with anguish week after week.

The sun was aglow with a rainbow halo.
I thought it might bring luck-but what do I know?

Opening my window for a simple breath of fresh air;
Instead, I get a cloud of smoke from the fire down there.

Chaos ensued as it always must do,
and now I'm choking on this hope-I never had a clue.

One foot in front of the other is getting harder every day.
I wish this smoke would cover me and take me far away.

Our hotel caught on fire after a myriad of other crappy things that have happened to us. I'm feeling especially sorry for myself today...but I'm sharing it here as there is no place for this kind of pity party in my real life. Too much to do.

TICK-TOCK

I knew you in another life, before I became me.

We worked just like a ticking clock, we helped each other be.

And as the seconds wind into hours of youthful memories,

Our friendship still gets me through the
minutes that feel like centuries.

BREATHE SLOWER

"Don't smile",
"Don't smile", he said.

When will you get that through your thick head?

"Don't cry"
"Don't cry", he said.

Then what;
Shall I just die instead?

A MESS WELL MADE

He screamed and protested with incredible force,
an agony which burned his throat and made his voice go hoarse.

I was moving with intensity as quickly as i could go;
Nothing else i offered him would ease his painful woe.

Finally, i rescued it from the depths of the noisy dryer,
My stress was at an all time plateau; it couldn't go much higher.

I rushed into his bedroom, making haste yet taking care;
For all his cries are quieted once he has Bear-Bear.

BLOODY SKIES

Betrayal swirling everywhere, it clouded up the sky.

The silver lining of a bloody cloud, releasing
crimson tear drops from her eye.

The ground cannot bear the burden of so much painful blood,

And so it crumbles like lifeless dreams,
unprepared for such a flood.

LONESOME DAY

What is it about right now,

that's got me furrowing my brow-?

I'm not sure why I feel this way.

It's such a lonely kind of day...

Simple but true. Feeling so lonesome today-and I'm not even alone...

ÂMES OUBLIÉES

Built upon a spongy moss; love songs of conversion
gracefully shrouded in green;

A road winding past passions, housing memories
dancing in moonlight-unseen.

Sweet beginnings: a place of healing for the lepers sent astray,

But then man did what men have done and twisted it their way.

The river border once symbolized hope in
the moments last remaining;

Have since been stained by all the blood of those
the establishment was detaining.

So many roles this institution of âmes oubliées had taken on,

But in the land of lilies and love the tower
lights still welcome the dawn.

This building is my Paris, the passion of
these memories a tiny scar;

Inside the heart of a city such as this, is a
place like Prison Saint Lazare.

French words: âmes oubliées=forgotten souls

NICKLE SMITH

I read this article on Prison St Lazare and its history and i thought it perfectly described Paris for me. Tragic and romantic, sometimes ugly but always changing-just like us...

DEMON SNACKS

So, this is how it feels to be ripping at my soul;
Tearing it to tiny shreds because it never made me whole.

I feel numb and terrified and absolutely depleted.
This cavern of hell is icy cold and always I feel so cheated.

I gave a sliver of love here and there; perhaps a dollop of trust.
A recipe for disaster which makes my heart combust.

I wish there was a haven safe enough to hide the gore;
The more i try to clean it up, the bloodier the floor.

I guess I have no option but to leave it on display;
For that's when all my demons come to poke at me and play.

WAITING ON A PARDON

My heart trickles blood like tears that burn
my hopes on their way down;

melting my loyalty into liquid fire and you the King will
hail above so royal, donning this ill-conceived crown.

Upon your head it rests like a costume piece on a fool.

How arrogant to think I'd bow to you-a man so cold and cruel.

From me you've stolen everything, broken
my honor and my trust;

So now, I release this love of mine and leave nothing else to crush.

THROW THE
FIRST STONE

Visions of grandeur, afloat the winds of destiny, slowly
POP like bubbles on the hot summer cement.

A melting popsicle of ideas leaving only sticky
remains of what it used to represent.

Memories of a poet changing. discolored like the creased
pages of a once tightly bound book, becoming torn,
over-used, and no longer given an honest look.

A life inspiring passion left its precious pucker upon a man's soul;

but once that passion flickered out, it produced a gaping hole.

He let the atmosphere take him where he would and could not go;

Determined he could light the fire and fill this burning role.

While wandering in the galaxy, he kissed the milky way.

He hugged the moon and danced with stars.
They begged for him to stay.

He traveled down below the sea to mingle with the beasts.

But even then, as time grew on, his loneliness increased.

Honesty, integrity, intelligence and grace;
is that much too much to ask for from my fellow human race?

His faith was slowly waning; no one there to spark the flame.
Every word or line he read just made him feel the same.

Finally, on a foggy night

he strolled on through the cloud. Suddenly, his
heart was caught by such a peaceful sound.

Familiar voices, siting phrases he'd grown to love and admire;
urging him to spread their word and help others to aspire.

UNMATCHED

The blazing sun
could never understand
how I could abandon its warmth for the touch of his hand.

The expansive stars
which dwell in the sky
grow increasingly jealous of the sparkle in his eye.

The salty waves are crashing and sounding their lament.
I never even said goodbye, just took my love and went.

A bond like this cannot be found floating along the sea.
It's a love that thrives inside the womb, that connected you to me.

I used to find my purpose in the treasures of the Earth.
But, this son whom I've been gifted with has
now surpassed their worth.

TIP OF THE ICEBERG

My eyes look just like icicles, or so, I've oft been told.

Tanzanite treasures that catch your gaze
but leave you feeling cold.

Easily wounded and caught off guard by the predators about.

So, I built this shiny wall of Ice to keep the evil out.

But, if you could find an entry point, or tiny
crack to just peek in; you'd find

a fire bright and hot is burning deep within.

SERPENTITIOUS USURPER

It slithered right in and darkened my door; then
everything I was, just wasn't anymore.

Skulking in shadows and offering up rope;
Sincerely wishing I would step right up and just abandon hope.

Darkness touches everything. It's sucking up the light.

Apathy must come to pass, it's time to join the fight.

Your venomous intentions always circling under toe;

have encouraged me to travel UP and leave you far below.

GRATEFUL FOR GRATITUDE

I share my heart; then, I read about yours.

How many sites can open up doors
and windows to self?
Things I couldn't possibly share with anybody else.

Privy to the secrets or healing that we find.
When I'm finished reading; I'll leave my thoughts behind.

An opinion for your liking, or perhaps, to your dismay.
That's the beauty of All Poetry;
we get rewarded either way.

Kevin is the man to thank for giving this for free.
In a world of cookie cutters, it's nice to get noticed for being me.

AIMLESSLY AIMLESS

I drink on this bottle, faster as I go, forgetting all
the somethings. I don't want to know.

I feel the weight upon me, reaching for my neck.

Responsibility crushing me; I'm such a **** wreck.

Just relax and take a break.

Leaving trouble in our wake, so, I plug myself in to the
media line and try to deflect and enjoy my high.

Release the tragedy on here instead;

by letting you see inside my head.

BABBLE

What's a word I haven't heard;
in hateful wrath or love incurred?

What's the purpose of a phrase?
In a sugary coat we now can glaze
over our half-truths and memories made.

Stunting action with a vicious tirade
of sentences strung in just such a way
to provide for you whatever they may.

Now creation weeps for a world that's lost
the ability to pay the cost
with deeds and heart and promises kept.

Coming up with this language while nature slept;
to communicate in an EASIER way, with the
things that I do, not the things that I say.

What's a word I haven't said
to communicate what's inside my head?

BELLOW

A black void of grief invites me in like an old friend.

I take a seat at the table of despair and
drink from my cup of solace.

I choose my song carefully from the angry juke box in the corner
of loneliness. I don't want to draw attention from the thief.

A taker of souls to the greater or maybe just other beyond.
I leave a tip for the empty waitress at the bar, taking
one last look in her eyes,-still nothingness there.

I step back out into the world of pretend and tie
my shoes of agony. Time to walk straight, walk
tall like it isn't weighing you down.

I saw you in the street again but knew you weren't
there. My friend, my shadow, your ghost.

So, I'll walk to your head stone again the only place I know
you really are. I'll cry my ferocious tears and scream my
worthless words so everyone and no one can hear.

Time is a thief. He is a liar, and he never gives back what he takes.

SOUL MEET

Two voices dancing entrancing through the static satellites
Hours upon hours sweet silly conversation delights.

Distance holding unfolding growing farther each day
Until words no longer quenched the thirst she couldn't stay away.

Anticipation growing, glowing, and igniting the spark.
A new world discovered in love; no longer alone in the dark.

Bodies mingling, tingling as they join together, at last.
No more waiting for forever. A future present from our past.

SUNNY SON

I awoke to the twilight and felt as if I were dying. The
achiness and swelling radiated through my bones. But,
I could not neglect his screams or the crying.

Slowly I raise myself out from under the weight of
my pain. Bitterness and self-pity fighting to win
but I cannot let them; this is not a game.

Making my way down the hallway he is calling for
me. Negativity struggling to envelop my mood but
I know it is me that he can't wait to see.

I open the door and a smile greets me right there. Loving
instinct now guides me on my way to his bed. I can't
wait to hold him or smell the hair on his head.

A tiny head on my shoulder a precious hand to my face. These
moments erasing suffering and putting my son in its place.

SCHIZ

I could turn a phrase or two for you and tell you what I always do.
I could make a list of all the things that make me feel I'm less.
But, what's the use of all these words when
we're making such a mess.

SAFETY GOGGLES

My head is foggy, it isn't fair.

It feels like something's in the air.

I really can't breathe. I'm gasping for breath.

Wishing and crying and hoping for death.

Why can't I see it, it's so close, it's there.

The voices singing louder, "Catch me if you dare".

I really shouldn't sleep this long, I'm standing straight and tall,

and when the nighttime falls again I'm staggering down the hall.

STRAIGHT JACKET

Give me a noose, because I won't even tie it, and
when the bough breaks I won't even try it.

ASHES TO ASHES

Take me home I've been gone far too long and everyone's watching and singing along. I'm shaking and quaking and missing myself, and when I got back I was somebody else. I don't really miss her and I hardly should lie, because my heart is an island and I can't swim and cry. I live in fear of the ashes of the bridges I've burned, the stories I've buried, the phrases I've turned. Sometimes they try to call for me when my heart just isn't there, and when I wake up drenched and cold I'm wallowing in despair.

TAKE IT OR LEAVE IT

I'll never be the kind of girl who oo's and ah's and plays the game.
Most the time I'm floundering in a puddle of shame and blame.
I could tell you not to worry, that surely I'm going to make it,
but sometimes it's just much to much to sit and try to fake it.